MW00896557

BLOCKCHAIN & FINTECH

A COMPREHENSIVE BLUEPRINT TO UNDERSTANDING BLOCKCHAIN & FINANCIAL TECHNOLOGY

2-BOOK BUNDLE

BY RICHARD HAYEN

Respective authors own all copyrights not held by the publisher.

The information herein is offered for informational purposes solely, and is universal as so. The presentation of the information is without contract or any type of guarantee assurance.

The trademarks that are used are without any consent, and the publication of the trademark is without permission or backing by the trademark owner. All trademarks and brands within this book are for clarifying purposes only and are the owned by the owners themselves, not affiliated with this document.

Disclaimer

BLOCKCHAIN

THE REVOLUTIONARY POTENTIAL AND IMPACT OF BLOCKCHAIN TECHNOLOGY IN BUSINESSES, FINANCES, AND THE WORLD

BY RICHARD HAYEN

TABLE OF CONTENTS

INTRODUCTION

The following chapters will discuss the purpose of blockchain technology and, likewise, the massive impact it's already had. First, we'll be delving into the history of the topic in order to give us a basic level of knowledge on why the technology exists and what its intended purposes even were. This is not an easy topic to tackle. It's very technical and it's very nuanced. There's also a whole lot to the history of blockchain, and the truth is that we aren't going to be able to even scratch the surface for the purposes of this book - not from laziness or anything of the sort but for the sheer fact that it's so intriguing and volatile that there's just too much to really go into within the scope of a book that's aiming to simply teach you the basics and essentially make a case for blockchain technology.

After we get through the basics of the technology such as the purpose and the history, we'll be talking about the nitty-gritty of the technology and its manifold uses. Heads up: there are a lot, even right now. There are only more to encounter too.

That will be the thing that we talk about after discussing the nitty-gritty and the uses, in fact; the numerous ways that this technology can be used going forward, and a few of the possible ways that it could change the world of business and finance entirely.

Lastly, we're going to be tackling the arguments against blockchain, and when it's really just honestly not a good idea to try to implement one. The truth is that blockchain is a revolutionary technology, but it's not always the best choice; there are many times where it's not even a good choice. I'm going to help you to identify those times so that you can make the most responsible choice for implementing a database however you need to, whether it be a blockchain or not.

There are plenty of books on this subject on the market, thanks again for choosing this one! Every effort was made to ensure it is full of as much useful information as possible, please enjoy!

CHAPTER 1: INTRO TO BLOCKCHAIN

Blockchains are an absolutely revolutionary technology. They're the basis of the cryptocurrency bitcoin. Blockchain is essentially a decentralized way of keeping up with information - normally transactions, but it can be used for essentially any purpose.

A deeper description of it would be that blockchain is a decentralized technological ledger. It holds transactions and information on thousands of computers all over the world. The transactions can't be altered retroactively, so it forms a trust-based system.

We'll go a bit deeper into the exact technology that is powering blockchain in the next chapter, but the important thing to take away if, after reading this book, you only retain one piece of information about this vital and exponentially growing piece of technology, is that blockchain is a database which holds a public record of digital transactions.

Designed by a person, or group of people, using the pseudonym Satoshi Nakamoto, blockchains are designed to be the apex of anonymity and decentralization in the modern world.

The entire idea behind blockchain was designed alongside the cryptocurrency bitcoin when Satoshi Nakamoto identified the problem that digital currency was not nearly as nuanced as physical currency in that it required - until the development of bitcoin and blockchain - a trusted third party in the transaction as a mediator.

Blockchain was developed in order to remove any kind of mediation or trust in the process of digital currency exchange (and digital information exchange in general), such that the currency could stand on its own as a viable means of exchange.

The intent was to make the notion of digital currency exchange far more peer-to-peer and less bureaucratic in nature. In that aim, Nakamoto succeeded in creating a system that would transcend the notion of arbitrary third-parties in currency exchange and move past it in order to establish a far more egalitarian mode of exchange.

The concepts underlying bitcoin and blockchain were conceptualized long before the actual development of the bitcoin and blockchain technologies themselves. They have roots in other digitally scare cryptocurrency technologies proposed by bitcoin's early adopters such as Wei Dai's early concept of b-money and Nick Szabo's suggestion of bit gold.

In its short history, bitcoin and blockchain have become immensely popular. The bitcoin project, alongside the first implementation of blockchain technology, was launched in January 2009 as open source software. Bitcoins are generated by mining, which is essentially verification of transaction blocks. There are rewards for verifying these blocks - fees related to the transactions, along with newly released bitcoin from each block. We'll get into the minutiae of these aspects in the following chapters, but what's important to note is that this is what incentivizes people to take part in mining bitcoin blocks.

Perhaps more impressive is the fact that the blockchain file for bitcoin specifically - meaning the size of all block headers and transactions combined - is around 90.6 gigabytes. Consider that every transaction is infinitesimal in size - at most a few bytes - and this number becomes massive. This means that this technology is a monolith for which there are few other words appropriate.

Another show of the technology's massive impact and huge presence is the fact that there are roughly 200,000 to 300,000 bitcoin transactions per day as of the time of writing in November 2016. Even a year ago, the average was around 150,000 transactions per day, and if we were to go two years back, the number is only five figures and is more along the lines of 80,000. This difference is huge, and the number is only going to grow as time presses forward and we find new applications for blockchain and bitcoin. It's worth noting that this is only bitcoin and that there are most certainly competing digital cryptocurrencies which have rather large bases of users themselves.

It's time that we stop doting on the broad concepts and get into the minutiae of the impact that it's had during its growth.

CHAPTER 2: THE IMPACT SO FAR

Blockchain started with bitcoin and, though it certainly didn't end with it, it's impossible to really quantify the impact that it's had without thinking about the way that the two have intermingled. It's also important, in order to understand where blockchain is going, to think about where it's been.

For years, people in the peer-to-peer community had been seeking a way to get rid of the trusted third party in peer-to-peer transactions. We already talked about how Nakamoto put their theory forth regarding how this could be done. Nakamoto would develop it and send the first bitcoins - 10 bitcoins to fellow cryptocurrency enthusiast Hal Finney - and would continue to develop it for the next year as the community grew rapidly, before disappearing into the ether.

The bitcoin currency grew massively and exponentially. The bitcoin community was not without its demons, however, and it's impossible to talk about the history of blockchain and bitcoin without considering its checkered past.

Bitcoin offered a certain level of pseudonymity. This is to say that anybody can start a bitcoin address. This isn't innately connected to them and their identity, so there aren't any prerequisites and there's no direct link between a person and their bitcoin wallet. So long as they took means in order to prevent such a link from forming, it's feasible to say that one could use bitcoin with nigh absolute anonymity.

The anonymity, thus, invited the technologies to be used for less than noble purposes. Websites on what is called the darknet, the dark web, the deep web, or other variants of the same theme offered innate support for bitcoin as a mode of buying and selling illicit substances and products. You could have analogized it to having the same amount of inanity and impersonality as giving cash with someone on the street. As long as there isn't a way to link that cash to you, you're fine.

Perhaps one of the largest of these was the Silk Road. The Silk Road was the largest internet-based drug marketplace ever, by far and bar none. Also for sale were things like counterfeit money and unlicensed back-alley weaponry. This site met its end when founder Ross Ulbricht was sentenced and the site seized. Since then, certain people have found bitcoins synonymous with illegal activity. However, this isn't accurate at all.

Though bitcoin and blockchain did rise, without a doubt, partly because of their pseudonymity and resultant integration into the underground drug market, they were actually very in line with a lot of people's worldview. The decentralized nature of blockchain technology led to people from both sides of the political spectrum praising it. Free market libertarians, for example, were very appreciative of the fact that it disconnected money from any sort of banking monolith and got rid of the hierarchy of traditional trusted-third-party systems. Socialists and anarchists, too, were openly appreciative of the fact that it dismantled the power of certain monoliths in the world of online banking for the most part. Political moderates both to the left and right generally saw it as a great advancement in technology and a huge boon to the world of digital currency exchange, which became far more personal with the advent of bitcoin and blockchain.

Likewise, a great many powers have picked up bitcoin as a valid method of payment. There are, for example, a large number of foundations that accept bitcoins as a donation. Wikileaks are a fantastic example in this regard. Also worth mentioning are the Electronic Frontier Foundation. in 2013, Overstock.com announced that they would start accepting bitcoin as a form of payment. After that announcement, many major brands like Microsoft, Dell, Time, and Reddit started to follow suit and accept bitcoin as a payment method.

This is a weird way of saying it, since what really happens is that the companies accept U.S. dollars which are converted by their bitcoin processing partners. Regardless, the support for the fledgling technology is still very much there.

2014 was a rough year for bitcoin. However, the blockchain technology which powered it saw a number of developments happen in 2014. The largest of these was a development to the technology which allowed individuals with the knowledge and desire to implement a ton of new technologies.

One huge part of these was the invention of blockchain APIs. These allowed developers to build on top of the blockchain protocol. Also important, and something we'll be getting far more in-depth with later, are the concept of smart contracts and programmable moneys. These allowed a lot of the elements of risk with cryptocurrencies to be mitigated in favor of manually programmed exchanges. These have been used by companies such as Empowered Law in order to transcend what was formerly possible with blockchain technology, allowing the blockchain to be used in a much more intricate way than before.

One of the technologies building upon blockchain technology is called Ethereum, which is another cryptocurrency much like bitcoin. It has a much more nuanced way of utilising the blockchain, allowing smart contracts to be implemented super easily. Another perk of Ethereum is that it can be verified in a much shorter time than can bitcoin. Where bitcoin is normally used for transactions at large, Ethereum tends to be used instead for tasks suited to labor.

Coming third in market share for cryptocurrencies is Ripple, stylized lowercase as "ripple". Ripple also utilizes blockchain in order to decentralize current payment methods. Ripple released a blog post called Ripple and the Purpose of Money that discussed the history of money and how modern architecture for digital payment is bizarre and prohibitive. Ripple uses their architecture as a means to espouse the idea of instant release of currency. Their purpose in existing is to revitalize an industry that is currently clunky and hard to work within. They say that the state of current digital currency is reminiscent of the email of the 80s - a bunch of different providers have a bunch of different set-ups for the same thing, and if you want to go outside of that then you're doomed. Ripple wants to make this a thing of the past.

Bitcoin has also spawned a huge number of other competing cryptocurrencies, generally called altcoin (or "alternative coin".) The fourth cryptocurrency in terms of market share is one such altcoin, called LiteCoin. It is structurally and functionally incredibly similar to bitcoin.

The decentralized blockchain has lent itself to the creation of hundreds of different kinds of cryptocurrencies, many of which being direct bitcoin derivatives. There are now over 710 cryptocurrencies usable in online markets as of the time of writing. They differ in terms of minutiae, and we'll get more into the exact details of that in the next chapter after we talk about what exactly blockchain is.

CHAPTER 3: UNDERSTANDING THE TECHNOLOGY (AND THE NECESSITY)

As you can tell from its intense growth, blockchain is a revolution. We haven't seen the least of what this tech is capable of. Regardless, like any revolution, the bold and smart thing to do is to be at the forefront. In order to do so effectively, it's imperative that you understand what truly makes up blockchain technology and how it is implemented.

We've already covered briefly what a blockchain is, but just to reiterate: a blockchain is a decentralized database which maintains sets of records.

These sets of are called blocks. Blocks are, by design, resistant to change and modification of data contained. This is furthered by the notion of decentralized consensus.

The blockchain format is such that each block is, as we've said before, a set of data or transactions. Every block holds so many transactions. These blocks are hashed and then made into a Merkle tree.

Every block has a timestamp and a hash which refers to the last block in the sequence. This forms what is quite literally a chain of interconnected blocks.

So what exactly is a block? In its most common usage, it's made up of a list of unverified transactions. These unverified transactions are verified through the act of mining, which is running a specialized program that parses an algorithm in order to verify a block. Within the bitcoin system, a block is verified every ten minutes.

For a long, long time, there was a problem in digital currency. It was referred to as the "double-spending" problem. The reason that it existed is because there's an essential divide between digital and physical currency: physically currency has a clear existence, right? You can see it, you can hold it, you can hand it off. You can verify that money hasn't been spent by the simple fact that it exists, right there in your hands or pocket or wallet. This isn't so easy with digital currency, since electronic files aren't unique. They can be duplicated. Because of this, spending a digital coin doesn't remove its data from the original holder.

The main means of this before the invention of blockchain was by something called a "trusted third party". This existed in multiple forms. One could, for example, describe the company PayPal as a trusted third party in a way, as it acts as a mediator for financial transactions between two people.

However, a way to use and exchange currency without having a trusted third party simply didn't exist - and that was the big issue, wasn't it? "Trust"? There had to be a system which would absolve people of having to strictly rely upon a third party in order to ensure that a transaction as valid.

Well, it would so go that there were various ideas and concepts of what could be done in order to fix the problem of double-spending, but Nakamoto was the first to really cover a possible solution in detail and was certainly the first to implement it. It was because of the solid implementation that bitcoin even caught on.

The solution that Nakamoto came up with was called decentralized consensus, which we've spoken about briefly and only in broad concepts and big words. To dive a bit deeper into the concept of the "decentralized consensus", all it is at its root is the notion that we divide up the responsibility of keeping up with transactions, verifying them against each other's version of a block and then coming up with a consensus as to the most relevant copy of the block. This takes the burden of verification out of the hands of some third party and instead puts it in the hands of several different acting computers.

The key concept here is decentralization. That's the entire concept underlying blockchain and bitcoin, too - getting rid of any kind of firewall which would prevent the users themselves from having as much control as possible.

In other words: once more, necessity was the mot[her]
invention, and it just so happened to birth us a beautiful,
mind-boggling system of innate checks and balances.

The necessity of such a system is found in the fact that it simply exists in and of itself. Trusted third parties are not a necessity. Think of it in these terms: the internet came along and decentralized information as we know it. Suddenly, everybody could take part within this system. The blockchain system allows people to take this third party out of the equation and do similar: decentralize trust and money much like the internet decentralized information.

I'd like to delve a bit deeper into the concepts underlying this technology though. For one, we need to talk about the type of cryptography which protects the blockchain. The blockchain has a specific level of protection which makes it incredibly useful and incredibly secure. This is essential to its decentralized nature. Because of this, anybody can view the blockchain but it's not open to security attacks.

This is actually absolutely incredible if you think about it because it means that there's a revolution of information and services coming up. But we'll talk about that when we talk about the implications of this technology.

Blockchain, too, is immutable. This means that it can't be changed or altered after it's been set to be a certain way, no ifs,

. You cannot change a blockchain. It is a

ger. It's like it's written in ink.

however, is not perfect. Nothing is resolutely

vould blockchain be? Especially considering how fickle technology has the habit of being in the first place. If it's immutable, then what do we do when there's a problem?

Well, to answer this question, we first need to take a look at the two major kinds of problems we encounter with blockchain technology. The bitcoin project has actually encountered both of these problems and shown us possible solutions to both.

The first problem we could encounter is a major bug in the chain that causes something undesirable to happen. If this happens, blockchain can't be changed, but it can be rolled back. Rolling back carries the same definition as it does otherwise in technology: returning the state of a program or process to where it was at an earlier point in time prior to an issue. It can be likened to a system restore, if you will.

The first time this solution was notably utilised was in August of 2010. On the 8th of August, Bitcoin developer Jeff Garzik noticed that there was a major issue in block 74638. What he described as "quite strange" was that a block somehow had ninety two billion bitcoins. What makes this so bizarre is that bitcoin has a built in limitation of only about twenty one million bitcoins. Not certain if you're a mathematician, I'm certainly not, but that's almost 91.98 billion bitcoins too many.

What had happened was an issue related to the programming of bitcoin and blockchain. Computers store value in certain pre-allocated spaces, and these pre-allocated spaces are only supposed to a number of x size. If some kind of arithmetic occurs that makes this value exceed (or undervalue) that which is technically possible, it creates what's called an overflow.

Somebody, in an act of partial genius and total malice, realized there was an exploitable bug in the software that powers bitcoin. As a result, they presumably wrote a custom bitcoin miner which utilized that exploit and produced an overflow. What happened was that about 91.98 billion extra bitcoin was generated.

The community was at first confused, but after a brief review of the glitch came to the conclusion that it must have been a hacker exploiting a bug. The bitcoin quickly came to the community that the best option was to essentially perform a system restore on the blockchain to a period before the bug was exploited.

This was done, and things were restored to relative normality. After the "restore", a patch was released that would fix the exploit. This is one of the few times that a rollback of such nature has been executed.

The problem with this kind of solution is that it becomes exponentially harder with public blockchains as the user base grows in size. This was not too difficult back in 2010 when bitcoin was not nearly as massive as it is now. However, if it were done today, it'd be exponentially harder than it was before.

The issue, then, with such huge blockchain rollbacks is that a consensus has to be reached. A consensus is defined as 51% of nodes, in the example of bitcoin at least, agreeing that the blockchain is one way or another. In this day and age, with the massive number of bitcoin users, it'd be nearly impossible to orchestrate such a task. Not entirely impossible, however. A ton of chaos would be generated in the process, and depending upon how fundamental the problem is, it may not be able to be entirely fixed. If it's a small and obvious exploit, then it may be able to be patched and fixed. Depending upon the severity of it, however - if it were some huge and extremely obscure mega bug - it may not be able to be fixed so easily, if it all. It can be likened to economic booms and depressions - you can patch up certain fundamental problems that cause these, but the likelihood is insanely high that it's going to happen again.

The reason that the 2010 blockchain rollback went so smoothly is the fact that the user base was much smaller and the bug was relatively easy to identify and correct. These are variables that make a rollback very friendly and easy. However, had they been slightly different, it might not have gone anywhere near as smoothly as it had.

The second possible major error that any major blockchain has a pretty high chance of running into is a little bit more convoluted than just a bug. Because of the fact that blockchains follow a consensus model, it's possible that due to certain factors (difference in checking algorithm, different software, and related causes) that something called a fork could happen.

There are two different and distinct kind of forks which could occur: soft forks and hard forks. Hard forks are significantly more catastrophic than soft forks and demand immediate attention. Hard forks will often require a rollback, so they aren't necessarily a distinct problem. However, not all rollbacks are the results of hard forks, so it's necessary to distinguish between the two.

Anyhow, to define the two separate forks:

Soft forks are when block acceptance rules are restricted compared to earlier versions of the blockchain. These are forward compatible and don't necessarily demand immediate action, if any, because of the forward compatibility.

Hard forks are when block acceptance rules are eased compared to earlier versions of the blockchain. Hard forks are not forward compatible. Hard forks are much bigger of problems than are soft forks.

It's easier to illustrate these concepts than it is to necessarily outright explain them, so I'll give to you an example of a hard fork.

In March 2013, there was a hard fork, and from March 11th to March 12th, there were two distinct blockchains. A bitcoin miner that was running version 0.8.0 of the software created a significant block. This block turned out to be incompatible with earlier versions of bitcoin. As a result, people running version 0.7 were actually rejecting the blocks made by those running version 0.8.0. This led to an entire new blockchain being formed.

There was mass chaos and confusion for a bit. In the interim between the release of a fix, the bitcoin miners using version 0.8.0 were asked that they revert to release 0.7.

In an attempt to fix the problem, the primary developers of bitcoin looked into what might have caused the older versions of bitcoin to reject the new blocks in the first place. Soon after, a patch was released. Version 0.8.1 made absolutely certain that there would be no blocks created that could even possibly be incompatible with older documents.

This ended up solving the problem altogether.

Hard forks can be terrible for infrastructure. However, depending upon the nature of the fork, they could occur naturally as a result of the userbase. In the event that the users are unable to agree on a certain convention and move forward in order to fix the blockchain, it's entirely possible that two distinct blockchains could be used, and - depending upon the circumstances - both might even be considered relevant and correct by the community.

Those are the two biggest issues that blockchain technology will run into. That's not to say they're the only ones, but they're the ones to be most aware of. Any sort of decentralized peer-to-peer program is going to have some kind of issue with keeping itself correct and updated, even if it's purely in a theoretical sense and absolutely safe-guarded against in implementation.

While we're discussing the actual form and implementation of blockchain, it's important that we recognize that there's more than one explicit and finite form of blockchain.

There are two distinct forms and paradigms for blockchain: public and private blockchain.

Public blockchains are designed and created so that they are accessible to anybody who has the adequate technology to access them. Generally, this simply means a computer and the internet. Future blockchain technology of course may demand more, especially depending upon how specialized the service in question is. We'll talk more a bit later about how more technologies could come into play in regards to blockchain. It's impossible to overstate how multifaceted this technology can be.

Anyhow, public blockchains have multiple benefits. The most obvious is that it's truly decentralized because anybody can take part in it. There is no third party. This is what blockchain was developed to be.

There's also the fact that when multiple organizations use the same blockchain, it can cut operational costs by the use of smart contracts.

However, because of the open ended nature of blockchain, this isn't the only option, and thus private blockchains also exist. Private blockchains are blockchains which are only accessible by certain people or firms.

Many people, including many authorities on blockchain, argue that private blockchains are an effective waste of resources because it's not truly decentralized. If you know the people that are going to be verifying a block, then what's the purpose of instituting a blockchain in the first place? it's effectively useless at that point to go through such trouble, because the principal appeal of blockchain - the decentralized nature which opens it up to being transparent and not corruptible - is essentially invalid. At this point, it'd be easier and faster to implement a normal database.

Bearing that in mind, I'm not trying to say that there aren't certainly advantages to private blockchains. There definitely are. For example, the transaction speed of a private blockchain can be much, much faster than a public blockchain. And privacy is built into the private blockchain - it's the entire purpose.

For the most part, though, there's not much of a reason to embrace private blockchain, at least in my opinion. You're certainly welcome to disagree.

Having talked about public vs. private blockchains, there's one more major facet of blockchains which needs to be covered: smart contracts.

We've spoken in brief about smart contracts earlier in this book when discussing the history of blockchain, but we haven't talked about what exactly it is or how it could be used. Smart contracts are ways to add code to any given transaction.

Let's break this down. There's a tea shop in the town over from me. Every time you make a purchase there, they'll put a little hole in a punch card. Once you have ten punches in the card, you get a free drink.

Every purchase and transaction is a contract, legally and financially speaking. Let's say that this tea shop offered the ability to buy through bitcoin and only bitcoin.

Smart contracts would enable a digital version of that punch card. Every time you make a purchase from that address, it would give you one free transaction from the address.

This is a very barebones and simplistic example but what smart contracts basically are is a way to give much more nuance to blockchain transactions. There's a lot more that could take place with smart contracts.

For example, gambling is made possible through smart contracts. People could pay into a smart contract, and the smart contract would automatically pay out to the winner or winners of whatever was being gambled.

You could program a set of money to only work on a certain store. If you were giving a customer store credit for a trade-in at a game exchange or technology store, you could have it programmed so that the bitcoin that you transferred them only worked at your store rather than anywhere.

In other words, smart contracts are a way to make financial transactions, well, smarter. They're not necessarily an intrinsic part of bitcoin or blockchain. In fact, they err far more on the legal side of things than the financial. That said, legal talk and finance talk go hand in hand because money is the undercurrent of pretty much everything ever in our society.

CHAPTER 4: THE IMPLICATIONS OF BLOCKCHAIN

So we've talked in brief about what blockchain is, but what does it really mean? We know the textbook definition, but what does it mean for society at large?

The biggest thing that blockchain means for society is decentralization. There are a million things that could arise out of decentralization, but the biggest thing that it represents decentralization of any given industry.

This means something very hazardous for the future of large companies. The thing about the blockchain model compared to the normal model for internet-based services is that the blockchain model is relatively impossible to track down. It naturally lends itself to any sort of peer-to-peer activity.

Think of it this way.

When you access a web server from a web browser, that server sends you whatever information it has to send you, which is then loaded and displayed within your web browser. If everything goes peachy then you'll type in the domain name, access the server via your browser, get information back, and be on Facebook or Google or YouTube or whatever in the matter of a mere second.

But what if there were an attack against one of these sites, or an official trying to take them down?

In the form of an attack, one could see a site be hacked into or its contents change. I can actually remember a point at which there was an insecurity in the web server of a government organization and somebody hacked into it and changed its content. So there's the first problem of a centralized copy: mutability. Anybody can go in there, theoretically, and change the content of whatever is being delivered from the server to the client.

In the form of seizure, one only has to consider the popular software piracy website Kickass Torrents which was seized by authorities and taken down within the last year. For a few months, where the site once sat instead was a sparse claimant page from the FBI saying that the site had been taken down for various reasons. This is where the second major issue with a singular copy and a singular distribution channel for that copy: fallibility. When you only have one means of delivering something and you only have one copy of that something, that something and that distribution chain are ripe to be seized. This example, of course, may or may not be controversial to even mention, depending on your stance regarding copyright laws and intellectual property, but this isn't the only manner by which a site could be claimed or seized.

The decentralized nature of blockchain and peer-to-peer technology prevents either of these from happening. It would be impossible to take down the entire blockchain network because there are multiple copies across multiple computers, it's self-replicating and self-referential, and there is little to no way that somebody could feasibly ever take the service off of the web no matter how bad they may want to.

There isn't a singular server for some zealous person or competitor to get a hold of, take down, and then completely ruin your business or application.

There's also the fact of the relative transparency of public blockchain. Everybody can view it but nobody can change it. This offers a lot of opportunities to actually, firstly, tighten up several processes in public administration and rid them of fraud, but it also allows them to make them free of corruption as well.

This could actually be a massive game changer in multiple ways that we'll talk about more in-depth in the next chapter, but right now, I just want to hammer in the concept of how important this whole notion is.

Transparency is going to be a massive reason that blockchain is used going forward. This allows people to know that something happening from person to person is truly supposed to happen, and allows one to verify that a transaction really did take place. The transparency works in the other direction too. Because blockchain is immutable, there is little to know doubt that what happened in the blockchain actually happened.

This is going to play a huge part when it comes to practical usage of blockchain technology because blockchain technology will allow the users to directly enter one thing or another into a blockchain and then it's on the record permanently, no redaction.

The fact that blockchain technology can be decentralized is key to what makes it so appealing for so many purposes. It's also why it could be a huge game changer and why so many people in the finance industry see it as a viable threat.

Blockchain offers the ability for people to quit having their hands held by trusted third parties and this or that institution; it allows people to finally be truly accountable for the things that they do and not have a mediary for any given action. This is why people love it. The autonomy that comes with it.

That autonomy scares people in power. That autonomy scares especially the finance industry, but also anything peer to peer that doesn't necessarily need a mediary party, because it could very well mean that it means the crumbling of said mediary parties.

This isn't too much of a concern at the moment, because blockchain in all honesty is still rather esoteric. The general person off of the street would be absolutely and completely lost if you asked them to explain blockchain and its uses. However, many things were once the same way. There was a time where e-mail and the internet both were incredibly primitive and only applicable to certain people. In fact, there was a time where even computers were primitive and hard to operate, and it wasn't that long ago. Before the Macintosh released in 1984, there wasn't really a consumer computer at all. But with that said, all it takes is time and the right platform to make something work.

Blockchain is going to change pretty much everything. The implication of blockchain currency is that we'll finally be able to get something that humanity has wanted since the development of the idea in the days of Athens: democracy. People are finally going to have much more autonomy over everything that they try to do and want to do. It's unnatural to have things be any other way.

Take currency, for example. The only reason that money goes through a central authority right now is because there's no other organized way. That's the long and short of it, to be perfectly frank.

Money represents something innate: value. Whether or not value is intrinsic is another discussion altogether reserved for late night talks of Marxist thought.

The history of money is so long and extensive that honestly going through the entire history of it is unnecessary and would take several pages to even give a proper cursory explanation. But here's the general way that money developed:

Money developed from paper receipts for stored grains. This would become precious metals which represented commodities stored somewhere. After a while, these precious metals began to have the abstract values of those commodities associated to them. This was the start of coinage. Paper money started in ancient China, and didn't hit Europe until around the 1600s because Sweden had so much copper that a copper coin with a decent valuation would be a few pounds and it was very impractical to carry around. Both paper money and coinage have carried over into our modern society, and were largely used to represent quantities of gold and silver and so on until the gold standard was largely dropped in the 1930s and 1940s during the midst of the Great Depression. Since then, money's value has become more of an intrinsic thing rather than a reference to the value of something else.

The point is that money exists solely as a way to give value to things. And for this reason, in order to have an organized structure of valuations of given commodities, we have to have an organized structure of money that can dictate such valuations.

This is the reason that every country has its own currency for the most part, but that these currencies are developed and distributed centrally: it's simply the best organized and most efficient way to keep a relatively orderly society with relatively well valued objects.

So the fact that we've managed to decentralize currency and move past traditional centralized distribution and organization of that currency is absolutely massive. It's impossible to overstate how fundamentally important to, indeed, human progress at large this could be if it catches on worldwide as a means of paying for things and determining values.

The implication of blockchain is massive decentralization, the likes of which we've never really experienced. I've said that this is the biggest thing since the internet, but if somehow a cryptocurrency massively takes off - if bitcoin continues to gain traction and becomes a predominant market force and eventually overtakes certain fiat currencies - if this actually happens, then it will be bigger than the internet. We've been searching since the dawn of civilization for a way to valuate things while retaining autonomy.

However, this also means a huge reallocation of societal power. A lot of people right now are benefiting off of the structure of fiat currency. We couldn't complain before, because it was the best option. The gold standard was dropped because it was a failure. Fractalizing the world's currencies and splintering them into more and more currencies that only work at this location or that location would actually serve to disunify humanity, despite the promises of free market types who say that fiat currencies are awful and a return to the gold standard is necessary rather than antiquated.

And the crazy thing is that despite this being such a huge step forward, there a lot of people saying that blockchain technology is overhyped. Like any technology, it has its limitations, sure. I'll be the first to admit that, humility being a key trait to any well-rounded person and all of that. But in my opinion, blockchain isn't overhyped. In fact, I'd argue that it's not hyped enough.

But perhaps I'm being overly optimistic with all of the "next step of humanity" talk. And if that kind of overtake by cryptocurrency were to happen, it would take a long, long time, and is unlikely to occur in any society where bankers have a lot of power because they have vested interest in fiat currency. With that said, there are a large number of undeniably amazing potential future uses for blockchain that can't be ignored. That's exactly what we'll be discussing in the coming chapter.

CHAPTER 5: FUTURE USES

Blockchain is a revolution. It's nothing short of a revolution. Once it comes into play and starts to hit the mainstream, blockchain is going to utterly and absolutely change everything that we know about finance.

In discussing the future uses of blockchain, it's important to recognize that not all blockchain data has to necessarily occur through a computer. The verification nodes may simply be run on computers, but there's no reason that anything else has to touch a computer.

You really have to think bigger than the current scope of technology.

Let's kind of break this down by industry in order to discuss possible future uses for the revolutionary technology that is blockchain.

Firstly, let's consider public administration.

One doesn't have to look far past any election to see that there are very apparent issues of corruption. Whether they're actual issues or inflated in scope and size due to the heavy emotional fragmentation and flaring which occurs as a result of elections doesn't quite matter. What leads to this worry in the first place is the overall lack of trust in the voting system and the feeling that it very well could be rigged.

This is actually the perfect job for blockchain technology. Because of its innate immutability and transparency, there's the possibility that blockchain could and would absolutely revolutionize the entire notion of voting and make it a far more transparent and altogether real process. This would work in parallel with politics to make people feel like it's less of a rigged game where the winners are already selected, thus getting more people to vote and be politically active in the first place.

Let's consider voting as a whole. There are different ways to implement voting. The most common manners are first-past-the-post and instant-runoff voting. Many people consider instant-runoff voting to be the most democratic but that's an argument for another book entirely.

How could we implement such a system? What would it even entail? Well, the blockchain would act as a ledger of every vote cast. Every time a vote was cast it would become part of a block. This block would be sent to the verifying nodes which would verify a block in set intervals. For this example, let's go ahead and use a federal election. Considering there are three hundred million people in the United States, let's assume a quarter of them are voting age and will vote at all. This gives us about 75 million individuals. Of course there are things like early voting but this is still a large load to bear for any system. Let's say that we verify a block every hour.

Every vote which is cast would be linked to a person somehow. The United States already has the infrastructure for this, in that every citizen has a social security number. We could use this social security number in order to link a vote to an identifier. However, these could be algorithmically hashed such that the information couldn't be traced back to the original holder of the social security number. This is important for protecting members of fringe political parties. For example, somebody who voted for the Communist Party USA or Party for Socialism and Liberation very well may not want their social security number linked to their voting preference because they could be put on a list or registry. This would function similarly to storing hashed passwords in a database.

Casting a vote would also work similarly to entering a password in a form submission: you enter your social security number and your vote is then linked to that number. This mitigates any chance at all of double-voting.

The social security numbers could be verified against a database to ensure that they exist. This may per necessity be checked against a centralized database of social security numbers in the U.S., but this already exists. There also may be an alternative method employed. The how and why of this doesn't matter too much for the purposes of conjecturing in this book .This is all just shooting at the stars in vague ideas of how this amazing blockchain technology could be utilized.

Anyway, every vote would be sent to the blockchain with a hashed identity. In this way, the blockchain becomes sort of a living, breathing "dictionary", to use a programming term. In programming, a dictionary is a set of keys and maps. The name is inspired by, well, dictionaries. In a dictionary, the key "apple" would map to the value of "a round fruit of a rose family tree, typically having a thin red or green skin." In our blockchain, the key would be a user's hashed social security number (or whatever) which would link to the value of their voting preferences.

Since a block is verified every hour, we would also mitigate the problem of vote counting and be able to get real-time election results. The blocks would be checked against one another every hour and then a consensus would be reached. This would be added to an election's blockchain.

For the purposes of efficiency and clarity, every particular sub-election within a main election may have a different blockchain. For example, the votes for a federal president in Wisconsin would go to a Wisconsin federal blockchain, which would then be verified and the values of which sent to the primary federal blockchain, which would then be verified. Meanwhile, the votes for the governor of Wisconsin would go to the Wisconsin state blockchain. This isn't 100% necessary but it would make it a much cleaner and more efficient system in the end.

I can imagine two ways to assure that you would have verification nodes among the general population. The first is to either pass legislation which actively enforces that internet service providers require their computer-owning customers to take part in the verification of the blockchains, or incentivize them to do the same. The second is to offer a federal stipend for people who are willing to use their computing power to verify blockchains. This would attract a great number of people because, frankly, who doesn't want an extra buck?

The key here is getting as many verification nodes as possible so that we have as many people verifying the blocks against each other as possible.

The advantages of this system are manifold. The first is that people would no longer be required to go to a voting location. So long as they've got a social security number (or whatever identifier that the system utilizes), they can reasonably cast their vote from anywhere: a home computer, a smartphone, a tablet, or even a library or a friend's laptop. This would heighten voter participation in the first place and get people to be more politically active than they would be otherwise. This would also enable people who don't have much time or freedom to go out and vote to ensure that they can.

This system would also reduce the chance of corruption, quite possibly to zero. All results would be verifiable by the general public if this were done by way of a public blockchain. Anyone tech savvy enough can look at every single vote that's cast, and anyone who cares enough to make sure their vote was counted correctly can find their vote in the public record.

This would be absolutely huge for public administration. It would completely alter the way that people view elections and make people feel much more connected to the political equation.

However, it goes beyond public administration. The blockchain can and will change the world of business, too.

A great many people have recognized the potential applications of blockchain for business. Blockchain integrates perfectly with the notions of a sharing economy, as well as the idea of an "internet of things". Before we talk about how it can be used for business, let's actually talk about these concepts and how blockchain integrates into them, because they're major concepts and they're certainly going to be coming up a lot more in discussions of blockchain in the near future.

The idea of a sharing economy is the relatively new idea that the internet be used for people to offer personal assets for certain services in lieu of traditional structures entirely dedicated to providing the same service.

Two prominent examples of sharing economies would be Uber and Airbnb.

Uber allows anybody with a license and a car to be a driver (with certain qualifications, of course.) This works great as a replacement to traditional taxi services because it allows anybody to do it, and not just somebody employed at a taxi service. Anybody wanting to make a quick dollar can do a few Uber drives.

Airbnb functions similarly, but instead of driving people around, people offer to host people in their homes. The idea is that they function differently to hotels because anybody with a home can host somebody, and it's no longer exclusive to the magnates within the hotel sector.

Blockchain integrates perfectly into the sharing economy because it's naturally geared towards peer to peer services.

In fact, a blockchain alternative to Uber already exists. It's called LaZooz. It's a ride sharing platform much like Uber, but it's completely decentralized. It's based around a currency called LaZooz. It rewards drivers, users, and miners with tokens called Zooz which can be used in order to receive rides.

And there's also more than one. Arcade City is another blockchain based ridesharing solution. It functions similarly to Uber, Lyft, and LaZooz. It has its own cryptocurrency as well, called "arcade tokens."

Now, on to the clunky concept of the "internet of things". It's actually relatively simple, but the name is clunky, so therein

46

it's clunky, right? Anyway, the "internet of things". The idea of the "internet of things" is that anything and everything can theoretically be made to communicate with one another and network against each other.

Let's take your kitchen, for instance. Think about your fridge. Your fridge could very much be smarter than it is right now. At the moment, you have to double check your expiry dates, think about what you can cook based off of what you have available, go to the grocery store when you run out of a certain object, and so on. You have to actively think about all of these things. The "internet of things" says "no, these things should all be interconnected and talk to each other. This should be simpler."

But a future fridge - and this sounds like something out of the Jetsons, I promise it's not - could theoretically keep tabs on a lot of this for you. Your cartons of eggs and gallons of milk could have RFID tags on them as opposed to barcodes, and these RFID tags could communicate with the fridge and give it updates and information about the product.

Your fridge could then know what's inside of it. It could say to you "hey, you've got chicken broth, pasta, and uncooked chicken breast. You could make some absolutely killer chicken noodle soup right about now," and what's more is that it'd be right, because the internet of things would allow it to keep tabs on all of this.

Or maybe your alarm clock could be linked to your coffee pot. When your alarm goes off, your coffee is already either ready or brewing. The internet of things is based around the idea that everything can be a little bit smarter and that the objects in your house can talk to one another.

In other words, it's the future. We're already seeing it manifest in certain ways. Consider Tesla cars. Tesla cars automatically download updates to provide new features and keep autopilot driving up to date.

The problem with this model right now is that these things will have to be identified and authenticated through cloud servers in a centralized manner, even if they're right next to each other. There are two possible solutions to this.

The first still requires centralization in a manner, but it's localized centralization. Instead of having every object connect to the cloud and then communicate with one another from there, it's feasible that there could instead be a local server within a house that every object could connect to and that thus could instead be the protocol by which these hypothetical objects spoke to one another. But firstly, that's an additional expense. There's also the caveat that if that server fails or fries, then your internet of things is virtually useless.

That's one thing we haven't really talked too much about, but that's one major appeal of blockchain: if one node fails, the entire thing doesn't go down. There are still several nodes in possession of the blockchain and that are actively verifying blocks. I simply becomes like that node didn't exist. The load and processes are adjusted, and life goes on, either without that node completely or until it returns and starts taking an active part in the verification of the blockchain once more.

Anyhow, if we're aiming to avoid the caveat of a centralized local server connection, then this is where blockchain comes into play. In its traditional manner, blockchain will allow these concepts to be decentralized and act as independent units that can connect and interact without having to be going through a centralized cloud server. This is a really big deal because this will massively simplify the way that the internet of things can manifest and also remove any element of third parties from the equation, even if this hypothetical third party is just a little white box with a processor and a touchscreen through which all of your "smart devices" connect.

This actually became a bit of a tangent, but the point I was trying to illustrate is that through the fact that it can impact and possibly override in many ways the quickly-growing "sharing economy", blockchain will revolutionize the world of business.

There are no shortage of ways that blockchain could change the worlds of business and finance as we know them. Blockchain, as potentially innovative as it could be though, does come with its fair share of drawbacks and potential limits. It's because of this that it's necessary to proceed with a fair amount of optimistic caution. These limitations are exactly what we're going to be covering in the following chapter.

CHAPTER 6: ARGUMENTS AGAINST BLOCKCHAIN AND WHEN TO USE IT

This chapter is actually going to cover the negatives of blockchain, and places where it doesn't have applications, or where the benefits of blockchain are essentially nil compared to more traditional methods of storing data such as information databases.

Throughout this book, I've been building blockchain up, but it's not at all a snake oil. It's not a fix-all for problems in technology, and it's not going to take over everything in one fell swoop. No, in fact - there are quite a few reasons why one shouldn't use blockchain, and quite a few instances where there's little to no advantage to using it in the first place.

The largest disadvantage to blockchain is that its transparency also comes with an innate cost. This could be a reason that it may never completely supplant the financial industry or usurp the current role of currency in our society.

The reason that the transparency could also be a liability is that, while it may reduce the probability of financial fraud, it opens up a window of opportunity for cybercriminals. This window of opportunity very well could be used in order to take advantage of the public financial information and exploit it and wreak havoc in general.

But beyond this, there are numerous other disadvantages.

One huge one is scalability. This is to say that we don't yet know how suitable blockchain is for high-volume trading. Consider the current state of bitcoin. Bitcoin isn't actually that big of a currency in a globally relative sort of way. But even at its current size and its current state, it requires a massive amount of processing power in order to be functional. A blockchain size is infinitely growing, and the fact that copies/updates of the blockchain are given to so many parties can actually be a bit of a stopgap in discussions about blockchain scalability. It will become so big that it's unwieldy or even impossible to continue developing.

Add on top of this the fact that one of the main appeals of blockchains is the fact that they're decentralized, and you have to recognize that a lot of the processing nodes aren't going to be running on supercomputers. They're going to be run on ordinary computers like yours or mine, and this means that if it's going to be meaningfully decentralized, there are only so many transactions which can take place in a given set of time and be verified because otherwise, these machines simply won't be able to handle the burden of the blockchain in terms of volume and complexity.

There's also the major hurdle that blockchains are kind of massive question marks when it comes to the legality of them in terms of currency. Most currencies in operation right now are Fiat currencies, meaning they're currencies which are created and distributed by governments as the primary currency.

If there continues to be a worldwide question in terms of the legality and the regulation of cryptocurrencies, then it's unlikely that financial institutions will be adopting bitcoin and related cryptocurrencies any time soon, and it's equally unlikely that they're going to be integrating blockchain technology into their existing infrastructures.

That in and of itself is actually a huge question. A complete switch to blockchain would raise massive concerns of the viability of integration. Many financial institutions have infrastructures built from years upon years of experience and status quo currency and status quo financial transactions. Replacing these systems is no small feat at all.

In fact, it's so incredibly parallel that implementing blockchain on a large scale would largely require a massive and complete replacement of existing systems and infrastructure. This is honestly just a massive hurdle that would be nearly impossible to overcome.

On top of that, the fact is that the current state of affairs in the financial industry is - in a way - far more energy efficient than any possible blockchain implementation. Bitcoin mining, for example, takes a lot of energy. A lot of energy. Bitcoin miners, as of the time of writing, try around 450 thousand trillion solutions per second. That's a lot of processing power. That's an absurd amount of processing power. That processing power doesn't come out of thin air, either. Knowing financial institutions, that cost is likely to be remunerated by society.

Not to mention that the processing power required to drive such high frequency trading as, for example, the stock market, or the incredible number of financial transactions occurring every single second between people, would be insanely costly at first. Though this cost would be compensated in due time due to the nigh instant nature of blockchain transactions, it would be terribly costly up front to both procure the capital necessary for such a shift as well as override and replace existing financial infrastructure.

This isn't to say that it's totally impossible, but it would be an incredibly massive expense.

One of the last major hurdles in blockchain technology is its very nature. It requires people to not only be interested in the technology that it powers, but also interested and invested enough that they are willing to dedicate time and computing power to helping it grow. Its decentralized nature is as much of a curse as it is a blessing.

Blockchain, especially in its infancy, requires a culture in and of itself. It requires that people at large pick up the technology and not only accept the technology, but they go further and refuse to reject it. The difference between these is phenomenal. It's easy to accept and nurture a technology. It's harder to be an active fighter for it.

Blockchain is as incredibly prescient and powerful technology but the reality is that without adopters, it's not going to go anywhere.

Consider the blockchain ride sharing solutions that we talked about earlier, LaZooz and Arcade City. They're focused around their own cryptocurrencies and offering a decentralized ride sharing solution. That's all well and good, but what are those cryptocurrencies worth if there's nobody that wants them? What good are the decentralized ride sharing solutions worth if there's not a person on earth using the service? Clearly, this is a bit of hyperbole, but my point is that cultural adoption is not only necessary for these services to grow popular, but it's vital in order for them to succeed and bring blockchain technologies to their maximum potential.

This isn't to say that blockchain is a bad idea. Not at all. Blockchain is one of the most revolutionary technologies since the advent of the internet. I sincerely hope that I haven't given the impression that it's anything other than that. There are so many possibilities which opened up with the creation of decentralized consensus and the development of new peer to peer possibilities that don't have to be watched or guided by a third party intermediary. It's one of the boldest things to happen in technology in a long while.

But with that said, there are some very real and serious considerations that need to be made about blockchain and its possible applications and projects.

That said, I'm far from a naysayer. There are a great many people out there that actively try to deride and break down new technologies and horizons because they dislike the notion of changed. Whether from vested interest, general discomfort, or misplaced good intentions, these people will try to fearmonger and say that blockchain isn't worth the time or the investment. This isn't true. Blockchain has opened up so many doors in technology and will only open up more.

Any and all problems which present themselves are incredibly likely to have tangible solutions with time. For example, the security issue can be fixed by using advanced cryptography.

Moreover, those things which don't have direct fixes are innate limitations of the structure of the concept in the first place. These things largely were known and acknowledged since the invention of the blockchain, and the fact is that for things which are limited by these constraints, blockchain plain and simply may not be the absolute best solution.

While we're on that topic, we need to discuss when to use and when not to use blockchain.

Let's think one last time about what blockchain is and what it represents. A blockchain is just a database that has multiple manifestations and verification steps. But because of its nature, it's best suited to large operations that involve many users.

If your process or venture doesn't have the potential to have a great many people using and verifying the blocks, then it's likely that you're going to waste time implementing a blockchain solution when a database would serve you just as well for what you're needing.

Earlier, I said that many times when you're tempted to use a private blockchain, it'll be a waste of time. I still think this is true. There are numerous individuals who will disagree with me, but I think it's undeniable that blockchains that aren't completely decentralized are self-defeating. Thus, if you think that you'd like to implement a blockchain that can only be accessed and verified by certain nodes, it may be worth reviewing your project and determining whether a simple database would meet your needs just as well. Chances are that it will, and will be more efficient than the blockchain structure would be in such a case.

With all of that said, don't let me discourage you from trying to implement blockchains if you think they're a good idea or will benefit your venture. Just be aware that there are plenty of times that blockchains may not be the greatest idea for a given data set. Even if it's constantly expanding, that doesn't mean that blockchain is the best idea.

Blockchain works best for keeping a ledger of data transactions that are not corruptible and are desired to be immutable. Note that this isn't necessarily financial transactions - these are any transactions of data that are set in stone. Events of the past that are finite and complete and done. If your data set doesn't meet these criteria, you most likely will not want to implement a blockchain.

With those provisions in mind, it's time that we pull this book to a close. I feel bad for ending the book on these sort of downers, but I built blockchain up for 5 or so chapters, so it was necessary to instill some sort of caution. Blockchain is a type of technology. This means that it's imperfect, and this also means it isn't a jack of all trades. It has its niches and its applications, and though they may be manifold, you cannot and will not be able to meaningfully apply a blockchain to quite a few things.

CONCLUSION

Thank for making it through to the end of Blockchain: The Revolutionary Potential and Impact of Blockchain Technology in Businesses, Finances, and the World. Let's hope it was informative and able to provide you with all of the tools you need to achieve your goals whatever it may be.

The next step is to start dreaming. As cliché as that sounds, this technology truly has so many applications. If you're a creative person and you think you'd be interested in coming up with ideas and applications for blockchain technology then by all means, do it. This world needs innovators. This technology has the opportunity to change everything, and I'm of the firm belief that it's going to do exactly that.

Like any technology, it has its limits. There are very real concerns concerning blockchain technology and the limits of what it can accomplish, but these aren't finite and aren't going to vary in every application. For example, just because scalability presents a bounds that will be difficult to pass in terms of blockchain applicability in the financial sector, that same issue doesn't necessarily exist in operations where the blockchain has a fixed size that it will eventually reach. The infinite nature of financial transactions doesn't apply to events where a finite bounds is presented, such as the very nuanced electoral voting example that I gave earlier.

That is to say that there are many applications of blockchain that haven't been thought of yet. Many people tend to think of it as an infinite ledger for financial transaction, but in reality, that may not be where it shines.

Blockchain's defining features are its decentralization and its relatively corruption free and transparent nature. These are the things that make it shine as technology.

There are certainly applications to be discovered where decentralization and transparency are amicable features, and these are the things which need to be sought out. It's appealing for infinitely scaling peer-to-peer networks, but it's just as appealing for those applications we haven't figured out yet where its drawbacks are mitigated and its numerous feats and positive qualities are amplified and pronounced.

But regardless of whether your application mitigates the drawbacks or not, what's important is that you come up with an application of blockchain to fix something broken or corrupt.

Actually, let me take that further: what I'm saying here is that blockchain needs you. It needs thinkers that are willing to slave over ideas and churn out new applications for this fledgling technology. This world is full of so much corruption. Blockchain offers a way around it; blockchain offers true transparency in the face of otherwise questionable practices.

If you're not a techie, then you can still do your part by promoting existing blockchain services. Seek them out. There are a great many out there, and even more popping up every single day. You can invest in up-and-coming cryptocurrencies (or ones which already exist!) or spread the word about the latest decentralized peer to peer whatever-it-may-be. All that's important is that more people - as many people as possible - become aware of the revolutionary potential of this technology.

FINTECH

THE IMPACT AND INFLUENCE OF FINANCIAL TECHNOLOGY ON BANKING AND THE FINANCE INDUSTRY

BY RICHARD HAYEN

TABLE OF CONTENTS

INTRODUCTION

Congratulations on purchasing FinTech: The Impact and Influence of Financial Technology on Banking and the Finance Industry and thank you for doing so.

The following chapters will discuss fintech.

What is FinTech? FinTech is short for financial technology. We'll go much deeper on the definition of it later, but for now all you need to know is that the world is in a state of revolution right now. This revolution could very well be as crucial as the first and second industrial revolution - if not more so. Already, we've seen colossal changes to the way that we interface with each other, with technology, with products and banks, and with money in general.

Money is the undercurrent for everything that happens and the FinTech revolution is at the very core of impossible-to-ignore societal changes that are going to - and indeed already have begun to - change the way that we see money as a society, that we trade, and that we work with and for each other.

There are plenty of books on this subject on the market, thanks again for choosing this one! Every effort was made to ensure it is full of as much useful information as possible, please enjoy!

Chapter 1: A Brief History of Money and Finance

Before we get into the current state of finance and where tech intersects with it, we need to talk about where money has been before. How it's developed and why.

It's very easy to fall into a certain trap of seeing money as an immutable object. Something which simply exists, like trees or clouds or water. But money is simultaneously more simple and more complex.

Money is as artificial of a concept as can possibly ever be described. Money is as man-made as boats or skyscrapers, yet it's treated with so much more reverence than anything else in the world.

Power, dreams, vivid hopes and the squalors of depression all coalesce at the feet of the almighty dollar. It hasn't always been this way, however.

Money is the by-product of scarcity and trade. People began to settle not too long ago in a period known as the Neolithic era, also referred to as the "new stone age". This era was absolutely crucial to societal development. This was the point in time during which we developed agriculture and began to settle into societies. The Middle East was the first region to see the sapling roots of civilization around 10,000 B.C., and the people who didn't settle there would continue to venture out nomadically. There's evidence which suggests that the majority of nomadic activity ended and people in general had settled between 4,000 and 2,500 B.C.

The thing which triggered the end of nomadic hunting and constant relocation was the advent of agriculture. The advent of agriculture is the single biggest event in human history, bar none. However, along with agriculture came the advent of certain things such as private property rights and ownership of commodities and materials.

The earlier and most barbaric form of trade commenced through a system of bartering. If I had 3 apples and someone else had 2 oranges, we could agree to such a trade. If I had 5 barrels of grain, I could trade that for somebody else's ox. Simple things like that.

However, at some point, somebody had the bright idea to create a new way to represent these values. We began to arbitrarily place value upon things and the fledgling idea of currency came forth.

The first use of currency was in Sumer, where there were receipts which represented a certain amount of stored grain. This would give way to metals which would be used to denote values for a stored commodity. This would actually form the basis for trade in one of the most historically prominent trade regions known as the Fertile Crescent - also known as the cradle of civilization.

After the fall of that form of currency came the first coins. These coins were made from precious metals and actually had innate value linked to the weight of that given metal. The metals were mined and weighed, then stamped into coins.

Paper money would be developed in premodern China. These stood for equivalent amounts of copper coins. These would become the standard in China and be mass-produced by the 11th century.

The medieval Islamic world is credited with the earliest uses of credit, checks, savings accounts, trusts, exchange rates, and banking institutions. In other words, the medieval Islamic world laid the groundwork for almost all modern economic fixtures.

Paper money became the norm in Europe by 1661 when it was introduced to Sweden, where copper was so abundant that its low value meant the need for massive coins. Paper money would take its place.

The central point here is that money is not intrinsic but rather is just a stand-in for arbitrary value. What exactly this value is depends upon your political slant, but the general American philosophy is that the value of money is relative to the demand for it, which equivocates to the value of a given commodity by the demand of said commodity. Thus the value of a given commodity can be expressed in a given quantity of money. Wordy and difficult to explain properly, yes, but it's certainly not rocket science, nor is it tainted with any air of academic exclusivity that many economists tend to get on their high horse about.

Money is simply that: money.

So this opens money, and the institutions which enforce and accept it, up to mutations. Just like money mutated from receipts representing a commodity to precious metals representing a commodity, it can mutate once more.

All money is is a way of representing a given arbitrary value.

A major way in which money has recently mutated was the dropping of the gold standard in the 1930s during the Great Depression. These values which previously represented stores of gold no longer represented that same thing anymore. This isn't to say that the value arbitrarily dropped - currencies compare against each other and have a relative value in and of themselves now. Some joke that the way that money has worked since the dropping of the gold standard is through some permutation of "market magic" or something of the like.

The point is that money is constantly evolving. It's natural for it to evolve. And right now it's undergoing one of the most major evolutions it's ever underwent.

The decentralization of information thanks to the internet has led to the introduction of one of the greatest source pools of information in human history, accessible from anywhere and everywhere. Nobody any longer is limited by their ability or location. People in rural areas now have access to much the same information as people in higher-density areas. People in Kenya can access the same website as people in America (provided the Kenyan has internet access.) What I'm trying to say is that the world is, for better or worse, a million times more open than ever.

With that said, let's take a little look at where things are now.

CHAPTER 2: WHERE THINGS ARE NOW

The current state of the world or finance is marked by large amounts of tragedy alongside gigantic bursts of progress. The tragedies are very clear: the worldwide recession has left many economies crippled, so far gone that it seems it'd be nearly impossible for them to recover. Indeed, things are tragic, and most tragic in the places where books about financial technology are at the backs of the citizen's minds. Many places are still feeling the reverberations of the 2008 financial crisis. However, alongside this are tremendous amounts of progress.

The invention of the internet and the smartphone have made banking accessible, well, not only at your bank. The internet represented the biggest decentralizing of information in the history of the world. It's far more possible than ever to have access to any information in the world that you'd like to.

We'll go more in-depth on the merits of financial technology and where it's ended up here soon. What's important to note is the immense and undeniable progress that are prevalent in the world of technology and finance. Everything is changing, and very quickly.

We were talking only a page ago about how the internet is more open than ever. This has opened up a whole new world of opportunity for change by relative nobodies.

Consider, for example, eBay. It was started by French-Iranian Pierre Omidyar. Though his father was a surgeon, he was from an unremarkable background. Well-off, sure, but there wasn't a brand-recognition to his name by any means. Besides, technology - especially the internet - has a beautiful habit of making that not matter.

In 1995, Omidyar began to work on "Auction Web", a venue for direct person-to-person auctions. It found its niche first with collectors of different items and grew from there. Its name would change to eBay in 1997. It grew exponentially from there into one of the largest web companies ever and one of the first examples of financial technology hitting the web.

The point of all of this is to say that there's an enormous potential in the world of financial technology.

Also, let's consider something for a second. Remember the whole 2008 financial crisis? Think about that old cliché "necessity is the mother of invention."

The 2008 financial crash led to the necessity of a new means for fundings and exchange as people began to grow distrustful of banks, financial advisors, and every other financial institution.

Out of this has grown a whole host of unique and frankly amazing technologies within the world of financial technology that are impossible to ignore and harder to give proper credit to.

CHAPTER 3: INTRO TO FINTECH

FinTech, or financial technology, is the all-encompassing term for all of the new technologies which are rapidly changing the technological industry. This is also a term used for all the things which drive innovation and provision of existent financial services. These are referred to, broadly, as financial technology solutions.

These solutions are generally defined by five differentiators.

The first such differentiator is sector.

Within the sector differentiator, there are bank solutions and insurer solutions. These tell which potential business sector they can be used for. Bank solutions are financial solutions that are intended primarily to assist and push forward the banking industry or specific companies or processes within that industry. Insurance solutions are financial solutions that are intended, likewise, for the insurance industry. Solutions for such industry are normally referred to as "InsurTech".

The next differentiator is business process.

This differentiator tells what business process specifically the technology provides or aids with.

One such example is payments. The payments process can include digital wallets or peer-to-peer payments - in other words, anything which helps the end-user with providing payment to somebody else.

Another business process is investment, wherein people are able to invest in particular ideas. This parameter includes equity crowdfunding. Another major business process is financing, which includes everything that helps with funding particular ventures, though not specifically business related. A major aspect of the financing business process is "crowdfunding", which we'll talk more in-depth about in its particular chapter but broadly refers to the outsourcing of funding to individuals all over the internet.

Next in the list of business processes is insurance. Financial technology involving this business process may include risk management software.

Additionally important is the advisory business process. This kind of financial tech can assist with financial advising, as the name implies.

There is also the cross-process business process. This involves financial tech which would, for example, predictively model an economy.

The last major financial business process is infrastructure. This means everything underlying the financial industry. A major part of this, though certainly not the only aspect, is security.

Beyond the business processes, financial technology can also be differentiated by customer segment. These distinguish between the various segments of people using the financial technology. This is generally divided into retail banking, corporate banking, private banking, life insurance, and non-life insurance.

Another major differentiator is interaction form. This details how the technology is used to interface between certain groups. The major forms are consumer-to-consumer (C2C), business-to-consumer (B2C), and business-to-business (B2B). This is relatively self explanatory but in order to illustrate, consider an online storefront that sells coffee. It would follow the business-to-consumer interaction form because the technology is fueling a transaction between the business and the consumer.

The final major differentiator is market position. This includes the distinctions of bank/insurer, non-bank/insurer or bank/insurer-cooperation, as well as non-bank/insurer or bank/insurer-competition.

Financial technology is important because it's nothing short of a revolution. Citigroup recently reported that approximately nineteen billion dollars of investment flowed into the financial technology sector from 2015 to 2016, compared to only around two billion dollars in as recently as 2011. That's a lot of money.

It's also the next big thing in Silicon Valley, where the push constantly is to find the next big thing. It's as beautiful as it is dangerous to be constantly pushing for innovation, throwing out old standards in favor of new ideas. And for as much of a threat as the banking and insurance industries tend to see the financial technology sector as, they have also served to greatly benefit those industries even in the short time that financial technology as a standalone sector has been an institution.

CHAPTER 4: FINTECH & TRADITIONAL BANKING

Financial technology is having a profound effect on traditional banking. As I stated earlier, previously banking options were relatively limited to what you could do in person. Financial technology is nothing short of a revolution, and this revolution just so happens to be a major threat to traditional banking.

First we're going to discuss how financial technology has already impacted banking and how it could impact it going forward.

Financial technology is poised to be a threat to traditional banking for the simple reason of convenience. However, some people think that this fear is baseless; indeed, some commentators say that financial technology can't override traditional banking for the fact that it needs it. Traditional banking is what our economy is based around, and it's the undercurrent of everything that exists right now as an institution in our finance-driven world. As a result of this, these commentators say that the financial technology industry is better off partnering with the existing traditional banking sector in order to take advantage of the infrastructure that they've already got laid down ready for use.

Many of these commentators are on the same page: financial technology is massive, and there's an incredible amount of opportunity therein, but traditional banking is going anywhere.

The financial technology sector has actually been a major boon to traditional banking. Almost two out of three respondents in the World Retail Banking Report 2016 reported using at least one fintech product. Eighty-eight percent of those respondents report trusting their fintech providers either somewhat or entirely.

The reason that traditional banking is scared of the financial technology sector is that fintech as a whole offers adaptability and innovation that traditional institutions simply are unable to meet. For example, customers report that the benefits to financial technology solutions in banking are ease of use, faster service, and an overall better experience.

Because of this, the overall innovation within financial technology and the broad adoption thereof is what is actually driving traditional banking institutions towards innovation and progress.

The fear of the financial technology industry isn't based in what has happened so far but rather what could happen. Fintech companies, in reality, have had an infinitesimal impact on the banking sector in terms of market share.

Traditional banking by and away still holds the vast majority of all market share in the banking industry.

One way or another, the financial technology sector is a huge deal, and existing banking institutions are doing their best to adapt with the innovation rather than fight against it.

Some are doing this only superficially and embracing fintech due to the fact that it's the next big "trend". Some, however, such as JP Morgan, are taking a genuine interest in financial technology, buying startups and trying to utilise the mind blowingly innovative technology that the fintech sector is producing.

The major way that the financial technology sector is driving change in traditional banking is by forcing the traditional banking sector to be far more customer-centric. Historically. the banking industry has been very poor about focusing on their customers. They've served simply as a financial stronghold, a place to store personal funds and - often - a place where those funds are manipulated through using them in the stock market.

The financial technology industry, however, is all about the end user. They have set a new bar for the banking industry to meet in terms of being consumer friendly and being easy to use. Because of this, banks are pushing each other aside in an attempt to meet the expectations of ease set forth by the fintech industry.

Alongside the fear of the FinTech industry are, as I said, many banks co-opting financial technology because of the numerous benefits. This has had a profound effect on the global economy, which is something we'll discuss in the upcoming chapter.

CHAPTER 5:

FINTECH & THE GLOBAL ECONOMY

Financial technology, too, is having an absurd effect on the global economy. It's difficult to encapsulate in one simple sentence, phrase, or even paragraph the profound influence that the financial technology sector is having on the global economy.

Firstly, it's impossible to really overstate the importance that the banking sector itself plays in the global economy. Banks are the single biggest player in the global economy.

We've already spoken at length about how the financial technology revolution has changed the face of traditional banking, but there's one aspect that we didn't really cover: the fact that financial technology has made it so that banks can eliminate jobs. Customers hardly have to visit physical branches anymore thanks to the fact that so much of what you would normally do at a physical branch of a bank - transferring money, making a deposit, checking your balance, making changes to your account - can be done from your mobile device now.

What's more is that there are even more jobs to be lost in the financial sector when new technologies come to fruition. Consider blockchain technology, which we'll talk more in-depth about later. Blockchain is an immutable ledger of transactions, in short. Once this technology takes off, there will be a large number of backroom and operations jobs at banks worldwide taken over by technology.

Another important aspect that will lead to job loss which we'll cover more in-depth later is called robo-advisors. If these are to become successful, many jobs in the investment banking sector will be decimated.

However, this is solely considering the implications for the financial industry.

Let's not forget that financial technology includes essentially all forms of e-commerce. This means gigantic implications, especially for the retail industry. The retail industry continues to announce massive job cuts in the ongoing years at physical locations. The fact is that these stores are simply served better by the financial tech revolution and the innate conveniences that it brings, such as e-commerce. It's far easier to buy something online and have it shipped rather than make your way out to a retailer.

While jobs are being lost in the traditional banking and retail sectors, jobs are being gained in the technology sectors as new startups in the financial technology industry are constantly formed so as to try to create new innovations. A great number of already existent companies, both technological and in the banking sector, are actually creating new positions dedicated to trying to concentrate on innovations related to blockchain and blockchain technology.

Financial technology's ease of use and easy funds of transfer from anywhere to anywhere has also led to the growth of major services such as Uber and Lyft.

A bigger part of this, and one that we'll go more in-depth with in one of the following chapters, is the way that financial technology has led to the overall simplification of administration and management of businesses. For example, consider that supply chain financing has been massively simplified for any firm that is involved in such a thing.

Perhaps one of the biggest factors of financial technology on the global economy is the creation of platforms that makes it easier than ever for people to start their own business.

At the root of capitalism and all capitalistic thought is the notion that with enough work, one should be able to succeed. Financial technology actually opens up this avenue for anybody with internet access. The previous barriers of the internet have fallen to the wayside and it's more common than ever for somebody to be self-employed.

There are two different ways that financial technology can benefit those people seeking to become more self-sufficient in terms of money.

The first is obvious. The breadth of financial technology services for the entrepreneur doesn't stop at Amazon and eBay. No, not at all. There are several online storefronts available for people to use as they wish. Examples of these would be etsy and Cafépress. There are myriad sites where people are able to set up their own little corner of the web and utilise the payment methods developed in the last 20 years, such as Paypal or Google Checkout, in order to craft and sell anything that they can really imagine. This is not a little feat. This is actually pretty incredible. These people before, to really have any presence selling their products, would have had to go through the process of developing a storefront - which, by the way, had a relatively chance of failing, all things considered - or their ideas falling to the wayside, selling only at craft shows or wherever they could convince to sell their products. Now, these people aren't hindered by such obstacles. There are, of course, some natural advantages - somebody famous will have a much easier time selling something than somebody not - but really, for all intents and purposes, the development of the internet and financial technology industry has gotten use the closest we may ever be to a manner of selling your products and goods without arbitrary distinctions - where the true metric of your product and the likelihood of your success is truly based off of the quality of your product and the degree to which you can promote it on social media.

The other manner is a tad bit more convoluted, but there are actually numerous mechanisms in place as a direct result of the growth of the financial technology industry which provide for a relatively hands-off way to make money. For example, you could sign up for an affiliate marketing site and get to work making blog posts promoting certain products. You'll get paid a commission from every purchase that your blog post directly leads to. After you have a certain number of posts, it becomes more and more hands-off. Though you'll need to post like mad at first, you could actually feasibly make only one or two posts per month after a year or so and make a reasonable amount. Every time you make a new post with an affiliate link inside of it, the amount of potential money for you to make increases because it, obviously, increases the amount of affiliate links you have on your site for people to click. You can actually partner this with the aforementioned storefronts in a new innovation called dropshipping, where your site acts as a middleman between your reader and a wholesaler. You sell an object for more than the wholesaler sells it, then forward the shipping information to the wholesaler. If this were a book about dropshipping, I'd go into a more detailed explanation as it's a tad bit hard to explain in cursory terms but the gist is that the customer doesn't know that you're sending the order off to a wholesaler. All they know is they're buying from your store for x amount of money, let's say $12, when the item from the wholesaler costs $8. You receive the $12 and buy the item from the wholesaler and ship it to the end user. You turn $4 profit in the end. Voilà: dropshipping in a nutshell.

And besides offering more autonomy for the individual to create their own online storefront, the innovation within the financial technology sector has led to the development of several innovations which overall reduce the amount of overhead involved within managing businesses.

Overall, the FinTech revolution only just started, really. Sure, we've made strides here and there since the advent of the internet, but a lot of the core services within FinTech, and the things that make it such a potential powerhouse for the world economy, are things that have only really been in development since the 2008 financial crisis. What I'm saying is that we're only just getting started. We'll talk more about where it could go later, but for now, it's just important to really take notice and care of the fact that the financial technology industry is revolutionising the global economy. Every day more, another thing becomes automated in the business world. Every day more, something else becomes streamlined and the whole process of owning a business becomes a little bit simpler and easier to handle. Every day more, a new initiative in FinTech is launched, a new idea for a service is created or a new fledgling company gets a startup loan. All of these things are important parts of the groundwork for a new world economy, completely shifted and transformed by the amazing innovations of the financial technology industry.

CHAPTER 6:

FINTECH & OUR PERSONAL LIVES

Financial technology overall is a revolution. It's hard, in fact, for people born after the year 1995 to imagine a world without PayPal or eBay. Financial technology has embedded itself so deeply into our personal lives such that it's almost impossible to imagine a world without its influence now. Such a world would seem nearly barbaric compared to what we're living in now.

I can think of a recent example where I was about to pay with a debit card but was unsure how much the account linked to the card had credited to it in the first place. Right there in the line at the grocery store, I was able to whip out my smartphone, open my bank's app, and check my balance right then and there.

This sort of ease has made financial technology a pillar of modern life. For example, anybody can check their bank balance at any time they like.

Also consider examples where you may want to buy something from a retail store that does price-matching, which is where a retail establishment will meet the lowest price of a competitor. It's now common practice for a great many people to actually check online retailers for the best price and then show that to a customer service representative at the retailer they'd like to buy the given product at. They'll then get the product for as cheap as the cheapest retailer.

This is such a common practice, in fact, that there are multiple apps dedicated to this exact purpose. One such app is called "ShopSavvy". You can enter the item you're searching for and you'll actually get a notification if a certain location lowers their price. You can also use this application in order to compare prices between multiple retailers such as Walmart, Best Buy, and Newegg. It's able to scan barcodes from your mobile phone's camera and compare the prices at a number of given retailers so that you can find the best deal fast.

Doing this before the era of financial tech would have been tedious to the point of hardly being worth it; such an endeavour would require going to multiple retail locations and, often, you'd have spent more going from place to place than you would have saved on the object in question (if you actually ended up saving much money at all.)

This holds another implication for the retail economy as well, which leaks down to the local buyers - it's much harder for retailers to price gouge any given object in the era of digital retailing and price matching, for the simple fact that it's incredibly impractical because people can simply check their phones for a better deal. The onus, then, is more on the manufacturer and distributor than the retailer to set the prices of a product, because the retailer is incentivized to price items competitively to similar retailers. This affects us in our daily lives because it allows us to get items for cheaper than ever.

That same implication also means that it's now much easier to live comfortably in a rural or semi-rural setting. So long as mail deliveries can reach your house, it's no longer hard for you to enjoy many of the same technologies that people living close to retail establishments can enjoy. You're only a click and a ship away from being on the same page as everybody else with many things.

We utilise financial technology so much in our daily lives that it's really difficult to quantify, and as the sector grows even larger and more ideas spring forth and more startups, well, start up, we'll only find ourselves using it more and more. The FinTech industry has already had a profound effect on our daily lives and it's earned an invaluable position in not only modern industry but also modern life.

CHAPTER 7: FINTECH & SUPPLY CHAINS

By now, you should have a firm understanding of the fact that financial technology is really, really great at taking existing concepts and making them better. That's the whole idea of progress in the first place, isn't it? Progression.

Well, financial technology did nothing less with supply chains. In fact, global supply chains could be utterly transformed.

The idea here is that financial technology companies could act as mediators to streamline the funding of the supply chain. The general assessment is that supply chain management in the past was about sourcing, producing, and delivering goods. However, it's now about funding, or using the supply chain as a way to obtain inexpensive capital.

FinTech companies in this context serve to streamline that process, too. They're now taking the place of banks which have traditionally dominated supply chain finance. They're overtaking banks for several reasons.

The first of these reasons is that the FinTechs are offering new and innovating business models. Not only are they refreshing but they also offer better ways of doing certain functions than the previously monolithic banks.

Another reason is that the financial technology companies are offering better digital interfaces and a multitude of tools for managing the supply chain, making it more hands-on and accessible than ever before to directly control and manage everything that you need to.

Yet another reason would be the relatively smooth implementation of financial technology companies' supply chain management tools. There are little to no "bumps in the road" per se when you're either integrating existing supply chain logic or creating new supply chain logic.

Financial technology companies are already taking up between ten to fifteen percent of the supply chain finance market and it's projected that their growth will actually accelerate as time goes on. There's promise yet for FinTechs in the realm of supply chain finance, and they're only going to catch on further as they implement more and better tools.

An analysis of the impact of financial technology companies on the supply chain finance sectors was published in the Harvard Business Review, written by Dales Rogers, Rudolf Leuschner, and Thomas Y. Choi. In it, they stated that multinational corporations like Apple and Colgate are already picking up financial technology companies in order to tap into capital that they hadn't had access to before.

They went on to discuss how simple FinTech has made supply chain financing, the authors of that analysis went onto state that financial technology companies were providing an integrated solution that underlies a process which begins with a purchase request and ends with payment to the payment of suppliers. They state that the nature of these systems allow the firms utilising them to greatly reduce the time in cost and labor of administering functions of the supply chain, due to the fact that they provide a streamlined structure for all necessary processes. To accentuate how easy the entire process has become, they state that joining platforms as such can be as easy as getting a phone application.

There's an incredible transition which has occurred. Financial technology companies have actually transformed the notion of supply chain financials and the structure thereof. Gone are the days of in-house departments dedicated solely to supply chain financing and management. Rather, this is all done under the umbrella of a third party's platform.

It's impossible, really, to overstate the prevalence and the importance of financial technology in the current supply chain finance sector. They've genuinely revolutionized the industry in a way which has absolutely no parallel.

CHAPTER 8: ROBO-ADVISORS

One major facet of the financial technology revolution is the advent of so called robo-advisors. The first of the robo-advisors were founded in 2008, when the recent major financial crisis went into full-swing. The initial idea was to rebalance investor assets while also giving them a modern high-tech way of dealing with their investments.

Prior to 2008, wealth management software was only sold to traditional human financial advisors who took advantage of the ability of technology to automate the work they'd otherwise have to toil away at. However, after 2008, the product started being given to consumers without any sort of middle-man or human financial advisor in the middle.

What robo-advisors do is provide portfolio management advice and take the place of traditional financial advisory. The robo-advisor services that consumers use in the post-2008 era of course utilise the same software and algorithms as do traditional advisors. In this, the robo-advisors are able to - at the most basic of levels - take the place of human advisors, at least in terms of rebalancing assets and accounts. What they aren't able to do is get involved in the more personal aspects of wealth management like taxes or retirement (at the moment, at least.)

Despite these relatively small shortcomings, robo-advisors are being seen as a major alternative to traditional advisors for an assortment of rather obvious reasons.

The principal reason for this is because robo-advisors, of course, are automated. Because they're automated, they cost a fraction of what it would be to staff or otherwise pay a human financial advisor.

On top of that, there's the possibility that investors will actually see higher returns using robo-advisors than they would see otherwise. This is because on top of the cheaper fees, they tend to have a number of exclusive automatic features like automatic rebalancing of portfolios, or tax-loss harvesting.

Bear in mind that robo-advisors aren't entirely abstracted from humanity. Many robo-advisors are actually just online advising firms that take advantage of automated technologies and programmed algorithms in order to take a lot of the hassle out of wealth management, as well as make it a cheaper horizon overall.

However, there are certain robo-advisors that actually offer access to a dedicated human financial advisor that will give you a living breathing ear to bounce ideas and help you manage your wealth altogether.

There are also better robo-advisors for different purposes. There are different tools for weekend investors than full-time investors and people who spend a large amount of time actively investing or otherwise taking part in the stock market. Every robo-advisor has different features, different account minimums, and different trade commissions.

Not everybody is going to have the same niche or the same needs when it comes to selecting a robo-advisor. If you're interested in robo-advisors, I'll be discussing a lot of the options currently on the market in the chapter on FinTech companies and startups, with an emphasis on the ones which are most promising for the layman picking up an Amazon book on financial technology out of sheer curiosity.

CHAPTER 9:

CRYPTOCURRENCIES & BLOCKCHAIN

2008 was a big year for the development of the robo-advisor industry. However, it was also a huge year for another fledgling industry.

Prior to the period of 2008 and 2009, there was only one way to store and transfer money digitally. This was by way of things called "trusted third parties". These include entities such as Paypal and Moneygram - companies which held an online presence and stored how much money that you, yourself, had at any given time and allowed you to transfer money through them.

The reason that these had to exist was due to a problem that, for a long while, went unsolved. This problem was known as the double-spending problem. To explain the double-spending program, let's draw a little line in the proverbial sand here: let's compare a physical money exchange and a digital money exchange.

Let's say that person A and person B are standing on a street corner. Person A wants to give person B five dollars. Since cash is a physical representation of money, person A is able to take five dollars out of his wallet and hand it over to person B. Person A then definitively no longer has this money because person B is now in possession of the physical entity of the money.

In electronic transfer, this couldn't happen. Because digital files can be duplicated, there's no way to be certain that the original file containing the money isn't on person A's machine.

In 2008, Yakamoto went to work at solving this problem so as to remove the element of trust from digital currency exchange and decentralise digital money transfer.

Yakamoto, that year, published a paper which set forth the notion of a digital currency called bitcoin, kept track of by something called a blockchain.

Bitcoin was the first of a series of currencies called cryptocurrencies, and is the first example of a decentralized digital currency as well as the first digital currency to solve the digital spending problem. Cryptocurrency refers to a digital currency which is kept track of in a decentralized manner rather than by a trusted third-party.

The way that bitcoin works is that an individual can make a new "account" so to speak, creating a new bitcoin address. Bitcoins can then be transferred to this bitcoin address from another. When this transaction takes place, it's recorded in the blockchain.

The blockchain is essentially a decentralized ledger of transactions. Though right now we're talking exclusively about the blockchain in terms of bitcoin, it's certainly not exclusive to bitcoin. Blockchain has a great number of applications and will be a massive part of financial technology and technology in general going forward.

Anyhow, this blockchain is made up of individual portions called blocks. These blocks contain a record of every transaction as well as every transaction held prior. Computers all over the world verify blocks against each other in order to come up with a best solution/best answer. This is called verification by referendum. This allows genuine transactions to be included in the block and be certain to go through while false transactions or attempts to "game" the system will for the most part be discounted. The only way that one could feasibly "hack" the blockchain is if someone were able to convince enough verifying computers that their version of the blockchain was the correct one.

In terms of bitcoin, a block is verified every 10 minutes, and contains a hash of the last verified block, allowing them to joined together and form an actual chain of blocks. Hence the name blockchain.

Blockchains are not limited to bitcoin however. Most cryptocurrencies use blockchain in order to keep track of any given transaction. But what a blockchain is, in essence, is a decentralized ledger of information. This information could be anything.

For example, consider the ride-sharing industry. Uber and Lyft were able to disrupt the entire transportation industry by offering an alternative to traditional cabs and taxis as well as a way to get a ride to or from places in as simple of a way as a few taps on your phone.

Many countries, however, have been working to limit the reach and scope of Uber and Lyft so that they don't disrupt the country's existing taxi services. In comes blockchain. A service called La'Zooz was started. La'Zooz uses tokens called "Zooz", kept track of by a blockchain. These tokens are used in order to reward drivers both users.

Because La'Zooz is decentralized, it can't be shut down or blocked or otherwise embargoed by governments or municipalities. There isn't a holistic entity that can be asserted as there is with Uber and Lyft.

In other words, blockchain is the protocol for decentralization. This means more than can possibly be said, going forward. Just like the internet was a revolution in that it decentralized information and allowed anybody to put out their input, blockchain is the tool for the decentralization of, well, everything else. Blockchain is the method by which you can effectively decentralize anything that you can think of, which means certain things will become unstoppable forces.

This is why libertarians and socialists alike are fans of the blockchain. It offers enormous potential for getting away from the monoliths of traditional capitalist business and move towards something bigger and better, straight from the hands of the people.

The possibilities of blockchain are truly endless, and play a huge part in the future of financial technology. We'll be going further into the possibilities that blockchain technology presents in the chapter where we discuss the future of FinTech in general. For now, we're going to discuss the incredibly pertinent FinTech industries of peer-to-peer lending and crowdfunding.

CHAPTER 10: P2P LENDING & CROWDFUNDING

In this chapter, we're going to be discussing two major forces in the financial technology industry, how they developed, how they're developing, and how they could develop.

The first of these is the idea of peer-to-peer lending, or P2P lending. This is a major part of the financial technology revolution. Peer-to-peer lending is the notion of lending money either to individuals or to businesses through any given internet-based service. These services work by matching lenders directly to borrowers.

The vast majority of peer-to-peer loans are unsecured personal loans. However, some of the largest amounts lent by peer-to-peer lending systems are lent to businesses as opposed to individuals. Secured loans are also possible through the system, which use luxury assets belonging to the borrower as collateral. There are many different luxury assets which may be used. Among these are jewelry, fine art, or business assets.

Peer-to-peer lending can also be used in order to fund student loans, payday loans, or real estate loans.

The interest rates on such loans are set in one of two ways:

1) The interest rates are set by lenders who compete to give the borrower the lowest interest rate.

2) The interest rates are fixed by the company hosting the peer-to-peer lending service after analyzing the credit of the borrower.

Peer-to-peer lending in America started in 2006 when the service Prosper was launched. Since then, the industry has grown immensely. After the 2008 financial crisis, people started turning to peer-to-peer lending more than ever for loans when banks were refusing to give out loans.

The two largest peer-to-peer lending services right now are Lending Club and Prosper. The two companies have serviced the lending of over two billion dollars - very impressive, indeed.

There are numerous benefits to the platform of peer-to-peer lending.

The first is that, since the service takes place entirely online, it has far less overhead than traditional lending services through banks. Because of this, investors will often see bigger returns. On top of this, borrowers often can receive better interest rates than traditional bank rates. The two combine to make this a fiscally responsible option for both lenders and borrowers.

Another factor which contributes to the appeal is that peer-to-peer lending offers the opportunity for investors who are interested in socially conscious investing to support the endeavours of people attempting to break away from high-rate debt as well people doing things that are morally good, and altogether avoid investing in people that are doing things that are immoral or otherwise detrimental.

Peer-to-peer lending isn't without its caveats, however. Peer-to-peer lending has been criticized due to higher default rates, since it tends to attract borrowers with low or no credit. Initially, it seemed that the default rates would be lower than traditional loans. However, this turned out to not be the case.

Another caveat is legal classification and lack of guaranteed repayment. This very well could make it an unappealing platform for many investors. The reason for this is that because in the United States, peer-to-peer lending is actually legally treated as investment. Thus, unlike depositing money in a bank, there is no guarantee of repayment in the event that the borrower defaults.

There's also a lack of certainty about the legality about such establishments. A legal case in California was held (Hellum v. Prosper Marketplace, Inc.) on behalf of all investors on Prosper between January 1, 2006 and October 114, 2008. The plaintiffs claimed that Prosper sold unregistered securities, which was against federal securities laws, and claimed that

Prosper operated as an unlicensed broker/dealer in the state of California. This certainly didn't slow the interest but does show that there's a tad bit of risk inherent in the industry. This risk, however, shouldn't be on the back of the investors but rather on the company themselves.

The other major thing to cover within this chapter is crowdfunding. Crowdfunding is tangentially related to peer-to-peer lending. While peer-to-peer lending is a form of direct lending allowed by financial technology innovation and the modern information era, letting lenders and borrowers circumvent traditional bank lending structures, crowdfunding is a form of raising money for a project or venture through a large number of people.

Crowdfunding has its roots in the idea of crowdsourcing - an information-age tactic of allowing a large number of people to contribute to a project or cause regardless of their origin or background, making it a large-scale community venture instead of a back-breaking venture for a single person or team - as well as historical tactics of raising money.

Crowdfunding outside the context of financial technology has roots in numerous different money-raising schemes over the years. However, crowdfunding in the context of financial technology is a relatively recent invention.

There were several one-off projects funded by non-standard crowdfunding ventures. Fans of certain filmmakers or bands or users of certain applications would often take part in campaigns to fund new albums or films or, in the case of the 3D graphics/game engine Blender, open-sourcing of existing technology.

The first major crowdfunding website was ArtistShare, launched in 2003. This site was created as a means for creative artists to fund projects they'd like to undertake by having the general public finance it, usually gaining access to extra content in the process.

After ArtistShare, several other crowdfunding sites would appear. The next major one was IndieGoGo in 2008, designed to fund independent projects. Kickstarter and MicroVentures would follow in 2009 and 2010 respectively.

Kickstarter would eventually take over the market and gain popularity due to its lack of particular focus and ease of use.

The Crowdfunding Center has identified two major variants of crowdfunding:

- Reward-based crowdfunding, wherein entrepreneurs or creative people presell a good or service in order to premiere a concept and procure capital to launch development without going into debt.

- Equity crowdfunding, wherein the backer will receive shares of a company in exchange for their pledged money.

The overall most common is reward-based crowdfunding. A massive number of projects have been funded thanks to reward-based crowdfunding. One major example of this kind of crowdfunding is Star Citizen, an online space trading/combat video game in development by Cloud Imperium games. Star Citizen has raised reportedly over $133,000,000. Another extremely noteworthy example is the Pebble Watch, which was funded by crowdfunding and raised more than $10.25 million.

There are numerous benefits and risks to this innovation of financial technology.

The first and foremost benefits are that crowdfunding enables the creator to raise their profile, offer marketing, allow them a forum by which they can engage with their audience, and a medium by which they can gain feedback on a project.

It's also a fantastic way to gauge the general interest in a project in the first place.

The most important way that it benefits the creator, though, is allowing them to procure capital whilst also gauging public support for a project. Normally, they'd have to go through several hoops in order to get the necessary funding for a project, and even then they wouldn't know for certain if it would even get off the ground, so to speak.

It's one of the foremost and most risk-averse ways of procuring venture capital.

However, the creator also has to bear the weight of certain risks. For example, failing to meet campaign goals or generate enough interest in the program could result in humiliation. Even worse, meeting a campaign's finance goals and create a substantial amount of interest in one's product and then being unable to deliver would severely humiliate a person and make them an effective joke within their given community.

Backers also take on a certain amount of risk. One can back a project and, often, get access to early releases or exclusive information or otherwise vital information regarding the progress of the project, but there's still no certainty that the project will be carried out to completion. Worse, tragedy could always strike: consider the game Project Zomboid. Though it wasn't crowdfunded, players were able to buy the game early and have access to early builds. However, the home of two of the developers was broken into. Two laptops were stolen which held the vast majority of the game's code. This set the development back by a huge amount.

There's a ton to both the institutions of peer-to-peer lending and crowdfunding, and when you think about it, they're both also only in their infancy with a long, long way to grow.

We're actually going to go more in-depth on companies that you can use for peer-to-peer lending and crowdfunding in the following chapter discussing financial technology communities, companies, and startups.

CHAPTER 11: FINTECH COMMUNITIES, COMPANIES, AND STARTUPS

Like most technological innovation, a great number of financial tech startups come from the seemingly infinite spring of tech startups that is the Silicon Valley in California. Silicon Valley is famous for having a sort of "start-up culture". Because of this, it would be incredibly short-sighted if not near sacrilegious to cover this massive hub of innovation without mentioning its communities, the major companies, and the fledgling startups. Let's go through these, one at a time.

Let's start out with the FinTech communities. There are entire hubs of people trying to stay up-to-date and on the cutting edge of this revolution.

The first one worth mentioning is FinTech Circle. This is one of the first and foremost forum communities for people interested in either learning more about or even taking up FinTech and doing something from within it. It's easy and free to sign up for.

In the same vein is NextBank. NextBank is a site where the top leaders in FinTech from all over the globe contribute their views and their ideas. It's a must-read for anybody venturing into FinTech. The central focus of the site is changing financial services through innovation and design.

BankInnovation is another site, similar to NextBank. It offers a forum for financial experts to posit their views on the financial industry and say anything they'd like to say.

It's incredibly important to be part of a community when you're following financial technology. The simple fact is that this sector is incredibly fast-paced. There are new things happening all the time and new innovations constantly. It's incredibly easy to miss a beat, and when you miss a beat in the song of FinTech, it'll be incredibly difficult to find a chance to come back in. FinTech isn't something you read a book about once and then understand. No, it's something that you've got to follow and be an active part of if you want to be an authority on the topic. With that said, the time spent reading and keeping up with it will certainly pay off. FinTech companies are shaping the way that investments are made and that finances in general are handled. Our metric of success in the Western world is finance. Your chances of being truly successful are much greater if you follow FinTech blogs and communities and stay up to date.

There are also some indispensable blogs that you absolutely need to follow and stay up to date on if you have any hope of keeping up with this industry.

The first of these is thefinanser.co.uk, also known as Financial Services Club. This site is effectively a repository for the thoughts and insights of FinTech magnate Chris Skinner.

When I say "magnate", I mean that this guy consults people on financial technology, speaks at events, and has authored a book on financial technology called Digital Bank. The guy is nothing short of a genius, and you are well-served if you decide to follow him.

Moving past the various communities, it's important that you know the most important FinTech companies. The reason for this is that finance, and manipulation thereof, is an innately dishonest game. However, using FinTech is one of the few honest ways to play that dishonest game.

Anyway, to be at the forefront of FinTech, there are quite a few companies you need to know. The specific company depends upon which aspect of FinTech you're looking into.

For example, if you were to look into cryptocurrencies, it would benefit you well to look into Bitcoin. However, bitcoin is decentralized and not really a company you can look into - you should, however, go to bitcoin.com in order to learn more about it. Also related to cryptocurrencies is Ethereum. You very much need to look into Ethereum if you're going to do anything involving cryptocurrencies. Ethereum, much like bitcoin, isn't so much a company as it is a mission statement. The goal of Ethereum is to create a cryptocurrency which takes advantage of smart contracts in order to add a much greater variety of decision making and autonomy to blockchains.

Or let's say that you were going to look into robo-advisors. Which specific company you should go with really depends upon your specific needs. Every robo-advisor is going to differ in its management fees and account minimums, and many offer promotions.

One particularly popular robo-advisor is Betterment. With Betterment, there is no account minimum. They do charge a .15% to .35% management fee, depending upon your balance. They also run a promotion wherein you get six months of free management with a qualifying deposit, which can be great starting out.

For weekend traders, Wealthfront just might be your best bet. Wealthfront has an account minimum of $500 and a flat management fee of .25%. However, they run a promotion where they will actually manage $15,000 of your assets with no fee.

However, if you don't like the sound of management fees, you could also consider WiseBanyan. They don't charge a fee for managing your portfolio at all, and have an account minimum of only $10.

Believe it or not, there's actually a robo-advisor out there too for your 401(k). Blooom is a great example of this. It manages your 401(k) for a flat fee of $5 per month if your account balance is under $20,000, $19 if the balance is between $20,000 and $500,000, and $99 for balances of $500,000.

What if stock portfolios aren't your thing and you instead wanted to look into peer-to-peer lending? Maybe you've got a small business you've been looking into opening for a while but want to see what the lowest possible interest rate that you could get on a loan is. There are myriad solutions for you in the realm of peer-to-peer lending.

We've already talked about the principal two companies when it comes to peer-to-peer lending. The first and foremost company that we need to talk about is Lending Club. They're the monolith in the category. They account for the vast majority of money that's been lent using online peer-to-peer services. Their site has the best user interface and the greatest number of third-party investors, as well.

The other major one is Prosper, which as we said earlier was the first American peer-to-peer lending company. The company has experienced phenomenal growth and has issued loans to the tune of about three billion dollars. Highly impressive.

For both of these, the average loan is around $14,000 with about a 14% interest rate.

We've also talked about crowdfunding as a major component of financial technology. Let's delve into some important crowdfunding companies.

First, let's look at reward-based crowdfunding. These sites generally operate based off of two models. The first model, all or nothing, means that when the fundraising period is over, the entrepreneur/creator only gets the funds if the goal is met. If the goal isn't met, then no money is collected. This is generally considered a safer option. The other mode is called keep it all, which means that whether or not the slated financial goal for the project is met, all funds go to the entrepreneur/creator. If the entrepreneur/creator is unable to meet the slated goals, it's up to them to refund the contributors.

The most prominent crowdfunding site is Kickstarter, aimed towards creative projects. Kickstarter is based on the all or nothing model, which means (once again) that if you don't meet the financial goal, then you get nothing.

Similar to Kickstarter is Indiegogo. Indiegogo allows a huge assortment of projects, and allows the user to choose at their own discretion which model they would like to follow.

For personal causes, the site GoFundMe just might be what you need. GoFundMe isn't incentive-based, which means that users don't actively get a reward in return for donating. Thus, it's better geared towards personal causes and live events.

Rally.org is oriented towards a variety of "bigger" causes such as medical, political, or educational causes. It follows a keep it all model.

If you find a loved one sick or dead, you can actually use YouCaring to crowdfund medical experiences or memorials or things or a similar nature. They charge nothing aside from payment processing.

Meanwhile, if you're looking to start a business, you may be interested in equity-based crowdfunding.

Equity-based crowdfunding works such that, in return for somebody investing a given amount of money, they're given equity in your company. Often, they're exclusive to accredited investors.

One of the foremost equity-based crowdfunding companies is MicroVentures. MicroVentures is geared towards tech startups as well as high growth companies. It has 28,000 investors who have invested a sum of seventy million dollars.

Another terribly important one is SeedInvest. SeedInvest is far newer than MicroVentures, having launched in 2011 as opposed to MicroVentures' 2009. SeedInvest is geared specifically toward technology startups in the early phases of development. Putting yourself out there on SeedInvest means putting yourself in front of more than 100,000 investors who are signed up to the site.

If your business isn't quite as tech-y as these firms would like for it to be, then you can look towards Invest Next Door. It's a site that serves specifically small businesses in America with equity-based crowdfunding.

Moreover, if you happen to be trying to start a business within a critical industry in America, or already have one that's in its growth stage, you may well look into Return on Change. It's geared specifically towards businesses which America desperately needs but doesn't have enough of.

There's also EquityNet, AngelList, and CrowdFunder which serve small and medium sized American businesses. They offer both equity crowdfunding and peer-to-peer lending solutions. EquityNet in particular has over 200 million dollars invested so far, while AngelList has 104 million and Crowdfunder has 100 million. These are very good and convincing numbers, certainly.

But really, it's a waste of time and space to attempt to go through every single established company in the financial technology sector. The reality is that the sector is so broad and has so many amazing things happening and so many amazing innovations constantly that it's nearly impossible to list all of them.

But the heart of innovation lies in start-up companies. With financial technology being such a fledgling sector with so much upward potential, it's imperative that we look at some start-ups with incredible potential.

One of the hottest start-ups that you need to keep an eye on is TransferWise. TransferWise is a peer-to-peer money transfer service that allows its users to very simply transfer money across currencies. What's amazing is that they manage to do these transactions at lower costs than traditional banks would be able to.

Another endlessly impressive FinTech start-up is iZettle. iZettle is a payments processing company. It provides businesses with a free card reader which plugs into tablets and smartphones. It's very similar to the U.S.-based Square which does much the same thing, but it's based in Europe and operates in Europe.

Fintech start-up eToro is incredibly captivating, too. It calls itself a "social trading network". Users of eToro can actually copy the trading strategies of other people that the users think are successful traders. People using the application are able to trade currencies, commodities, indices, and CFD stocks.

All in all, the financial tech industry is based largely out of Silicon Valley, which means that startups are its heart and soul. It's important as a follower of the financial tech industry to always keep an eye out for new startups and newfound potential.

It's impossible to really write a book about FinTech without discussing a lot of its key players. Hopefully this chapter has covered the vast majority of the vital pillars in the industry, as well as companies to watch out for. Now, we're going to talk about the future of FinTech before we bring this book to a close.

CHAPTER 12: THE FUTURE OF FINTECH

The financial technology sector is nowhere near its peak. Rather, it's only just started. There are already a ton of new ideas that are just waiting for consumers to embrace them, and beyond those slated ideas, there are a million new possibilities.

One such new idea is the notion of peer-to-peer insurance. Peer-to-peer insurance takes conventional insurance and aims to save money by reducing overhead costs and inefficiencies and increasing the overall transparency of the process of buying and having insurance.

Also worthy of note are the potential future applications of blockchain technology. There's been a spike in interest around things like blockchain insurance, blockchain remittance, blockchain lending, and things of that nature. The decentralized nature of blockchain appeals to a great many people and could be a factor of creating new peer-to-peer programs in the future that completely turn the traditional structures of insurance or lending upside down.

But I'm not here to conjecture and, frankly, you're not here to read me conjecture. You want solid data on where FinTech could be in the next couple years. Well, allow me to assure you that FinTech is not a phase. The best possible thing you could do right now is invest in the financial technology industry. It's only going to grow and grow some more. But where to invest?

We've talked before about how the financial technology industry is seen as a massive threat and a possible disruption to the banking system and financial institution and, well, this is absolutely correct. The truth is that while the FinTech industry would benefit greatly from partnering with existing institutions, it's more likely that they simply don't need the infrastructure these existing institutions have to give. They're better served, in a business sense, by completely disrupting and overriding them.

Whether they override them or not likely doesn't matter too much. They are a massive disruption to the industry in general and are likely going to usurp them eventually. Financial technology and everything within the industry is a means to democratize the institution of capital. That is to say that previously banks were the gatekeepers of capital. If you wanted to transfer funds, you went through a bank. If you wanted a loan, you went through a bank. If you needed help paying medical bills, you went through a bank. The entire financial tech industry is working to reduce the amount of power that any given institution has while also streamlining certain processes and putting people more in control.

This whole notion is the root of the peer-to-peer aspect that a lot of the programs and firms seem to share. They're trying to take the power away from the banks and, though not necessarily put it in the hands of the people at large, give people more overall autonomy in any given financial decision they make, as well as more freedom to make those financial decisions from anywhere - be it at home, at the park, or across the country on vacation.

CONCLUSION

Thank for making it through to the end of FinTech: The Impact and Influence of Financial Technology on Banking and the Finance Industry, let's hope it was informative and able to provide you with all of the tools you need to achieve your goals whatever it may be.

The next step is to use the information I've given you. There are multiple ways you can do this.

The first is obvious: you use these services to your advantage. For example, if before, you didn't know that robo-advisors were available to you to help you make wise investment decisions, now you do. You can shamelessly invest in the stock market and - hopefully - see some great returns off of that.

There are multiple utilities discussed in this book that can help you to take your money (or lack thereof) and create much more out of it. Granted, not all of it is about that. That wasn't the purpose anyhow. The purpose was to teach you all about the revolution occurring right now within the financial technology sector, and all of the ways it affects you and the world around you. However, you can certainly take advantage of this knowledge in order to do something great for yourself.

The other way you can use this information is to invest in this industry. There are new ideas taking off or trying to settle their roots into the ground constantly. There's no reason you shouldn't be at the forefront of this.

At one point in the book, we talked about equity crowdfunding. This is one avenue particularly worth looking into when it comes to the fintech sector.

As with any sector cluttered with start-ups, they aren't all going to succeed. In fact, a great many of them may not. Scratch that - a great many of them will not. But for every dozen copycats or clones, there's one idea out there that has an amazing foundation and basis. All it's awaiting is the funding, the opportunity, and the support to go forth. That could be you.

Or if you don't have the means to invest but you're a programmer, you could be the one developing. Surely at this point in the book, you've had an idea or two pop up for something you could do, even in those subconscious corners of your mind that seem to stay cluttered when you read. Provoke those. Build upon them. Research and figure out if they've been done yet. If not, then you can be the one to start it.

Also, it's absolutely necessary that you keep up to date on everything to do with the FinTech industry. As I said, this industry waits for nobody. There is a constant hustle. Billions of dollars are being invested into it each year, more and more with each passing year as new prospects and start-ups pop up promising to revolutionize everything. If you miss a beat, then you're going to have a ton of catching up to do.

Keep up with as many FinTech related blogs as you can, and join as many FinTech related communities as you can. Money changes; money evolves; money is malleable. This means that it's not necessarily a science. Some things never change. Oxygen will always have the same number of atoms. Two plus two will always equal four. The value of the dollar will not always be the same. It's not a constant of the universe. It's a man-made thing. The way to keep up with man-made things is to keep up with men. You owe it to yourself to get in with as many financial experts or people even interested in the world of finance, so that you can talk out any questions or concerns and stay up-to-date on current events. The entire world is impacted by the littlest of things in the most bizarre pond ripple you can imagine. Little things can make a world of difference in the economy, and it's important that if you care about the FinTech sector, you stay on top of that in communities of people watching for the same sort of thing.

In closing, financial technology is a revolution. If I've said it once, I've said it a million times. This is as big as the start of the internet. This is as big as the Macintosh in 1984. This is as big as The Beatles. This is not a wave you want to miss, and there's no reason you shouldn't surf it.

Made in the USA
Middletown, DE
17 March 2017